I am
for how you have look
over me over my
years.

Much Love,
Alex V. Eott

MEASUREMENTS

DO YOU HAVE A RULER?

BY ALEX V. SCOTT

"For I can do everything through Christ, who gives me strength."

"For we know in part and we prophesy in part, but when the perfect comes, the partial will pass away. When I was a child, I spoke like a child, I thought like a child, I reasoned like a child. When I became a man, I gave up childish ways. For now we see in a mirror dimly, but then face to face. Now I know in part; then I shall know fully, even as I have been fully known."

1 Corinthians 13:9-12, ESV

"Let no one deceive himself. If anyone among you thinks that he is wise in this age, let him become a fool that he may become wise."

1 Corinthians 3:18, ESV

"An intelligent heart acquires knowledge, and the ear of the wise seeks knowledge."

Proverbs 18:15, ESV

"The Lord detests dishonest scales, but accurate weights find favor with him."

Proverbs 11:1, NIV

Dedication and Acknowledgements

This book is dedicated in loving memory of my grandfather, Rev. Willie L. Scott, who passed away on January 19, 2018. He will be remembered as my mentor, spiritual leader, and best friend. He had discussions with me about him writing his own book, but passed away before it could be written. Because of the spiritual knowledge and encouragement he provided me since I was a child, I gained the courage and strength to write this book.

I would also like to acknowledge the people who helped shape me into the man I have become. My mother, Pat, raised me to always be me, no matter how different I saw things. My older brother, Adrian, for constantly treating me as an equal. He made me feel equal to others in life by telling me I was his big brother, even though I've always recognized him as who he is, my big brother. Rev. Wells, for adopting me into his family, physically and spiritually, at a time when I was in need of a father figure. My grandma, Beulah, who was instrumental in teaching me the strength in loving others unconditionally. Lastly, my beautiful wife, Shené, and our wonderful children, Kirra and Alex Jr., for allowing me to be me, and supporting me as I strive to lead our family. They have given me purpose in an area of my life where purpose was needed.

CONTENTS

Introduction 1

<u>Spiritual Development: Infant Stage</u>

Chapter 1: What Are You Building? 7

Chapter 2: Not a One Person Project 19

<u>Spiritual Development: Toddler Stage</u>

Chapter 3: Do You Have the Tools? 37

Chapter 4: Measure Twice, Cut Once 51

<u>Spiritual Development: Young Adult Stage</u>

Chapter 5: Guess Work 71

Chapter 6: No Quick Fixes 79

Chapter 7: It's Not Level 87

<u>Spiritual Development: Adult Stage</u>

Chapter 8: Imperfect, Not Finished. 99

INTRODUCTION

In the *Apology of Socrates,* Plato writes about the uncomfortable relationship Socrates has with the Athenian political atmosphere. Within those writings, Plato characterizes Socrates as a "gadfly." In the Book of Jeremiah, the prophet Jeremiah had a message to deliver to Egypt.

> *Egypt is a beautiful heifer, but a gadfly is coming against her from the north.*
>
> Jeremiah 46:20, NIV

Within these two writings, I would like to emphasize the significance of the term *gadfly*. A gadfly represents various flies, such as a horsefly, botfly, or warble fly. One of their purposes is to bite and annoy livestock. Imagine a horse standing in one spot sleeping and grazing for hours. The gadfly eventually annoys that horse out of that comfortable spot, into another spot. I write this book in hopes that it would act as your "gadfly."

Over the past couple of decades, I have had my share of "gadfly" moments. I am married with two children, work as a full-time firefighter, and graduated from Belmont University with a Bachelor's degree in Theological Studies. But within those life situations, I have had stages of becoming comfortable. I went through periods of my life where I felt stagnant, but oftentimes liked the spot that I was in. As annoying as my gadfly moments became, they forced me to move into different and sometimes uncomfortable spots. Finding a new spot forced me to experience things in life that shaped me into a leveled individual. I no longer live based on the comfort of the spot that I am in. I gained knowledge within the shifting. I hope to share what I learned in those experiences within this book, so that you may utilize them to possibly move from spots you may have become too comfortable in.

In 2012, I finally gained an understanding of the purpose of gadfly moments. My wife and I decided to sell our home and move to a new city. It wasn't a new state. It wasn't even hundreds of miles away, but it was a new location. I was comfortable living in the surrounding area of Nashville, TN, and now I was shifting to the Mt. Juliet area where I was not familiar with anything. That moment forced me to examine myself in an extremely different way. My priorities had to change. As a family, we decided to purchase a fixer upper. The challenges and lessons I learned in my life while remodeling our home structured this book. I had to take on challenges and look back over my life in a variety of ways, but I found myself in the process. I was annoyed by being "bitten." I was forced to find different spots, but individual knowledge was gained.

I am a firm believer that there are two ways for us to experience life's lessons. There are those who have to go through the experience, and there are those who learn from seeing, hearing, and critiquing others' experiences. I'm thankful to God for allowing me to share my experiences, and pray that I am annoying enough to force you to choose a different spot, allowing your experiences to assist with continuous growth. No matter who you may be, what your religious beliefs may be, or what stage of your life you may be in, remember there is a purpose for the gadfly moments in your life.

There are four stages of Christian development that are designed to unveil instructions to better live our created life. Our journey is continuous, but for you or I to develop as Christ instructed us to develop, we must pay attention, evaluate, and understand what decisions need to be made to grow and potentially unveil our purpose.

Spiritual Development: Infant Stage

Brothers and sisters, I could not address you as people who live by the Spirit, but as people who are still worldly-mere infants in Christ. I gave you milk, not solid food, for you were not yet ready for it. Indeed, you are still not ready. You are still worldly. For since there is jealousy and quarreling among you, are you not worldly? Are you not acting like mere humans? For when one says, "I follow Paul," and another, "I follow Apollos," are you not mere human beings?

1 Corinthians 3:1-4, NIV

The infant stage is about thinking only of oneself. If an infant is denied the things desired, he or she will raise a rumpus. Babies seek their own. Feelings are easily hurt and are often jealous. A baby lives to be served, never to serve. Drinks milk and cannot eat tough meat. Cries, but never sings. Tries to talk, but never makes sense. These infant characteristics are so prominent in the lives of many church members. They have been born into the family of God, but have failed to develop spiritually. They are spiritual babies - carnal Christians.

Chapter 1

What Are You Building?

Building objects is observed as an important part in childhood development. Having the ability to build assists with teaching skills like vocabulary, math, and balance. That development improves a child's motor skills and intellect as they grow into adulthood. At some point, we, as adults, lose the desire to continue building. That change renders us helpless to the direction others may choose as proper development. The building that has taken place for the development of the masses is beneficial, but relying on others, silences the unique creativity that rests inside of each individual.

In the fall of 2006, my wife and I were shocked to have the opportunity to have a house built. Having a house built was viewed as one of the great accomplishments of our young lives. We were five years into our marriage, our first child, Kirra, was three years old, and we felt this was the right decision to make to facilitate our plans to have another child. The process of having a house built was exciting, but stressful. If you have ever experienced owning a home, you understand it is mostly about budget. We picked out everything we agreed upon within our budget - fixtures, lighting, cabinetry, and brick color. There were a number of decisions made to design the house the way we desired. We would drive by our house weekly to see what phase had been completed and take pictures.

After seven months of waiting, we were able to move in and make our new house our home. Life in our home was exhilarating. We celebrated every holiday and birthday. We made up days to celebrate. Our second child, Alex Jr., was born and we could see our plans coming together. I was enjoying being a firefighter and a youth minister. My wife was a teacher. We talked about having a boy and a girl when we were planning our life together, and those plans came true.

As the years passed, the newly built home we designed and felt was one of our greatest accomplishments, turned into just a house. Our relationship struggled. We couldn't discuss dinner without arguing. Our finances struggled. We made money, but had none to buy what was needed. We began pointing fingers at one another as the cause for the issues we were facing. No one could do anything right. My wife and I agreed about one thing. We both felt like we were tip toeing on eggshells around each other. We were in a confused position and about to reach our breaking point.

In 2012, we hit a huge turning point. My wife's vehicle was repossessed. It was embarrassing, but enlightening at the same time. The truck driver that came to repossess my wife's vehicle was a friend I went to high school with. Not only were we losing our vehicle, but the image I assumed I had was leaving, too. That was an emotional day. I remember looking into my wife's eyes and thinking, enough. We decided we couldn't keep living in denial. We had been going through gradual changes years prior, actually looking at our debt issues and openly discussing how we drifted apart as a couple, but the repossession accelerated our change. We were living to satisfy the perception of society and others. We had remodeled our first home and remembered being a couple that desired to use our hands and create. The opportunity was never available in our new home, so we tried desperately to modify it to satisfy our craving of creativity. Somewhere along the way, we conformed to the idea to follow the gradual steps of society.

When we reach adulthood, society plants a seed in our non-experienced minds that the image of adulthood involves you purchasing a starter home, then the "next step up" home, and then an even bigger home. It was a foolish and unwise decision to build a house to fit an image we perceived was placed on us, but it was our decision to dupe ourselves into believing our egos. Our original plans were not completely our plans. They were the plans we thought would allow us to fit into our view of society. We were sinking as individuals and as a family in that house.

In the gospel of Matthew, Jesus was teaching a large crowd and his disciples. Jesus stated:

Therefore everyone who hears these words of mine and puts them into practice is like a wise man who built his house on the rock. The rain came down, the streams rose, and the winds blew and beat against the house, yet it did not fall, because it had its foundation on the rock. But everyone who hears these words of mine and does not put them into practice is like a foolish man who built his house on sand. The rain came down, the streams rose, and the winds blew and beat against that house, and it fell with a great crash.
                                                                Matthew 7:24-27, NIV

Through those struggles and gadfly moments, we rediscovered who we were as individuals and as a couple. We tried to make that house fit what we had discovered about ourselves, but it was built for the delusional image we had created for ourselves. It was time to move. We agreed to sell the house and haven't looked back.

In a society where we are presented with the notion that what people think matters more than what we were created to be, desire is created to build a life based on the perceptions of others. We are inexperienced, infants, in the game of life. Society dominates our perception of individualism. In 2018, there were over one hundred social networks worldwide with billions of users. There were also over three thousand magazine brands worldwide for us to consume. No wonder we have a difficult time figuring out who we are! Our lives are constantly judged and measured by content and others. How do you figure out who you are, or dig through all the misinformation to find yourself? I suggest the stages of denial, trial, and identity. Jesus explained it this way:

If anyone would come after me, he must come deny himself and take up his cross and follow me. For whoever wants to save his life will lose it, but whoever loses his life for me and for the gospel will save it.
Mark 8:34-35, NIV

Denial

Jesus clearly states you must deny "you." How is that possible? It involves you withdrawing from fellowship with the *you* that has not grown in the direction or purpose you were created for. If you continue to live life following those who have no direction, you will eventually end up nowhere, feeling like you are nobody. When you are asked who you are, your answer should not be your name. You must navigate your life back to the life God created you for, allowing yourself to discover your purpose for living. If we need the detailed purpose of a product, do we take it to someone who knows a little about it, or do we take it to the manufacturer? The Creator of all things is more than capable of providing the created *you* with the purposes of *your* existence. Denying the *you* that keeps routinely making choices to sin against God is a huge step to turn *your* life over to God, allowing *you* to be discovered.

Trial

Taking up your cross involves you putting yourself on trial. You become the prosecutor, defense, jury, accused, and victim. There is only one Judge. Taking yourself to trial forces you to reevaluate your life decisions. Every good or bad decision you have made will be discussed, examined, and reexamined to see if you are in line with your created purpose. The concept allows you to analyze the path you've chosen and whether your decisions line up properly with how you define yourself.

Hard to tell? Here's an example. You may want to be a baker, but everything you bake comes out of a premixed box. The premixed box contains a specific mixture, serves a specific purpose, and has a specific result created by someone else. Taking pieces of how others' live their life and trying to mix it with your perception of life can result in you becoming some form of the persons you copied. *What were they mixed with?*

You must be real about who you are and what you are capable of doing - mixing your life together from scratch. If there is a life you want to pursue, it takes time and effort to accomplish that life. You will find yourself guilty of ignorance if you continue to go through life assuming you can plead your way out of every trial you experience in life. Getting on the right path takes you having full knowledge of who to follow and why they are worth following.

Identity

This final stage positions you to choose which path best fits where you would like to go until the end of your existence. Your identity is not defined by your fingerprint, social security number, or credit score. It is determined based on who you decide to follow. There is the world and there is God. You may believe it is possible, but you cannot serve both. We assume we can be a part of both based on how we choose to live, but the decision is in the hands of the one with the most power. No, that's not you.

We have the misconception of "straddling the fence." There is a reason there are two sides to the fence. No one has the ability to balance their life on that skinny pole of separation. You will eventually fall or turn to one side or the other. Let's use common sense. Straddling a fence, over time, will become painful. I also would advise you to consider questioning what type of fence you are trying to straddle. You did not create you. You cannot define you. A side must be chosen.

The examination process of denial, trial, and identity will either lead you back to your original spot, or lead you to a more defined understanding of being created. You must be open to looking over your past decisions and journeys to allow the process to unveil understanding. Having an idea and working toward living out your full potential should push you toward building a better you. The house you should build is you, but it would be foolish to keep building it to sink. There is one thing you must do to navigate your way to figuring out who you are. A plan!

Do You Have a Plan?

As children, we learn to do things on a schedule. Eat, sleep, and play time is scheduled by parents or guardians. That scheduling provides us with a sense of being aware of our time. Children struggle with planning out the day, but as we mature and gain more understanding of responsibility, we grow in our knowledge of the importance of planning. It allows us to take lead in the direction of our lives and others. So, we must be transparent with ourselves when evaluating whether we are prepared to lead. Ask yourself these critical questions:

- Have you been preparing yourself mentally, physically, socially, and educationally for the position you are being positioned for?

- Are you living your life in an exemplary way, not contradicting the example that position must uphold?

- Do you have the support of your family or suspected following?

- Is there anyone actually following you or are you bullying your way to the front?

- Is the position you are positioning for actually your calling?

You want to be the leader of your life, but have no clue where you are going or have confidence in your decisions. Why do you think others should follow you? Get in line with the other followers and understand you are not ready to lead. Remember it is okay to let someone else takeover. There is the saying, "We don't plan to fail, but we fail to plan." I'm a believer in both. Apostle Paul writes in the book of Romans:

Do not be conformed (in likeness) to this world (present time or age), but be transformed (changed) by the renewal (renovation) of your mind (carefulness), that by testing you may discern what is the will of God, what is good and acceptable and perfect.
Romans 12:2, AMP

Paul mentioning the word *conform* represents the understanding of knowing what is worldly and what is not. You can't change something unless you have knowledge of different options. When you become aware of the decisions that create turmoil in your life, you must make changes. Constantly choosing to make decisions that cause your life plans to stay the same is reasoning to change course.

Proverbs 17:10 (NLV) states, *"A single rebuke does more for a person of understanding than a hundred lashes on the back of a fool."* Since the reason for failure is known, but hidden for the benefit of your worldly image, the desire to follow a plan that leads to purpose is deemed voided. You cannot change a journey if you willingly sabotage the changes. Why make your images for others more important than living out a fulfilling purpose? Do not allow the child in you to dictate the choices necessary for development into your adulthood.

My grandfather preached planning to me at a young age. He would tell me to write down what my plans were on a sheet of paper and evaluate those plans yearly. The idea was to review the list and see how God is moving. This is what made the list important. It identified whether I was in line with God and my progress. It helped me stay on a proper path and highlighted God working. Things I checked off were found to have meaning. Those things that were left, were evaluated as off track or transferred to the next yearly list.

I would forget what was on the list months after writing it, but that is the point. It's not for me to control. It was me communicating with God, while God was orchestrating and revealing His relational guidance. Of course, I didn't understand what my grandfather was sharing with me until I decided to get serious about my life. I decided to stop trying to build my internal house with my own truths, and turn my life over to the Truth. Basically, God knows what He is doing. Do you?

Gadfly Moments:

- *If, to live you had to live a balanced life, would you survive?*

- *Will your dysfunction sabotage the survival of someone close to you?*

Chapter 2

Not a One Person Project

Do you ever feel alone even though you have people around you daily? In 2013, I experienced loneliness like I never had before. We finally sold our house and decided to move into an apartment to get our lives in some type of order. It was a huge undertaking after all the misdirection that had taken place while in the house. We moved into the apartment during the summer, so the transition was not really hectic. We signed a one year lease, planned to save and pay off as much debt as possible, then purchase a fixer upper house.

A year didn't give us much time, but we were focused. We could work on putting the pieces of our lives back together or continue to drown in our undesirable circumstances. Being a firefighter and my wife being a teacher allowed us to have beneficial time as a family over the summer. Family bonding and adjustment to living in a small two bedroom apartment was moving quickly, but was soon interrupted once school started back. With my wife starting back teaching and kids back in school, I was at the apartment a large portion of some days alone. Little did I realize I would experience anxiety during my alone time, and be forced to look at myself from a different perspective. I was prideful, trying to be the man, so I expressed feelings to no one.

The days my family was away at work and school, I felt lonely and that feeling opened me up to vulnerable realities about feeling unwanted and misunderstood by those present in my life. I began to examine how my life developed into what it had become. During my childhood I struggled with anger. I had a serious temper that would boil over into destroying things. I got kicked out of daycare for biting a teacher, continuously throwing chairs, and constantly fighting with other children. I knowingly acted out against those in authority up into my high school years, almost being expelled. I saw it as a small issue, but the feelings about growing up without a father present intensified. I thought I had dealt with the absence of my father, but I came to realize that I had buried that part of my life. The way I dealt with it was to not deal with it at all. I treated it as though it was not a big enough issue to burden myself with.

My father left when I was around a year old. He left my mother, with some support from family, to raise two young boys. The connection with my father was never cultivated, but it shaped me as I became an adult. My childhood was filled with him popping up for a day or two, making promises, not keeping promises, and then leaving for years at a time. I remember telling my brother not to believe any time my father was supposedly coming to see us.

There were numerous situations that bugged me about how my father treated us, but I chalked those up to him being him. Growing up hearing that fathers being absent in the home was a common theme in the black community, caused me to become numb to the circumstances of the relationship. I did not understand how that period affected my character. I measured myself being a husband and father to how I felt about the presence and absence of my own father. Struggling with acceptance of others and trusting others was revealed. This period helped me discover the recurring anxiety issues I experienced growing up. I felt I had no one I identified with, as a young man, to help me develop into any perception of what a man is supposed to look like. Anxiety overtook me, developing the mindset to only trust in myself.

I liked being around people, but didn't trust getting to know them. I didn't want to deal with the disappointment. I had already decided that they wouldn't deliver before giving them a chance. I was unknowingly sabotaging my life. I functioned as a young man needing others, while at the same time wanting to be alone because it was safe. Not trusting in others became a comfortable way of living. There was no one to disappoint me and I had convinced myself it was less disappointing to prevent trusting others by not allowing the cultivation of trusting relationships. The realization hit me like a ton of bricks. I had become what I constantly reminded myself I didn't want to become, my father's son.

Paul explained this concept:

> *I do not understand what I do. For what I want to do I do not do, but what I hate I do. And if I do what I do not want to do, I agree that the law is good. As it is, it is no longer I myself who do it, but it is sin living in me. I know that nothing good lives in me, that is in my sinful nature. For I have the desire to do what is good, but I cannot carry it out. For what I do is not the good I want to do; no, the evil I do not want to do—*

this I keep on doing. Now if I do what I do not want to do, it is no longer I who do it, but sin living in me that does it.

Romans 7:15-20, NIV

I had finally reached the point where I was strong enough to endure the stronghold of my childhood. God's unveiling of my character guided me to the truth about my circumstances. The house we sold wasn't the issue. The decisions we made didn't create my issues. My wife wasn't my issue, and my relationship with my father wasn't my issue. Living as though I was alone and had control over my life was my issue.

God and the individuals He positioned in my life were always with me, and I never acknowledged their presence. I had to become more aware of God's presence and aware of the presence of those around me. Their caring and loving presence was evidence contradicting the loneliness I assumed I was living. This period helped me to begin building a transparent relationship with God, and strengthen my relationship with my wife and children. I became a different person. The "Father" I craved attention from had been present my whole life. My favorite scripture growing up and still today is: *"I can do all things through Christ who gives me strength." (Philippians 4:13, NIV)*

Only after going through this period of anxiety, did I fully understand the meaning of the verse. I really only cared about the first part of the verse, which stressed what "I can do." The key is understanding that it is "through Christ" you are given the strength to do what it is you are doing.

This Is Heavy

There is a phenomenon called the "size weight illusion." It involves the view that two objects of the same weight are perceived differently in weight because one object is smaller than the other. The perception is that the larger object is heavier because it is expected to contain more material. Once both objects are lifted and the larger object is determined to not be as heavy as first perceived, the perception is shifted to the heaviness of the smaller object, and how it seems similar in mass to the larger object.

Our natural reaction to the burdens that hinder our lives is to tackle or resolve the issues that appear to be largest and perceived to be heaviest on our shoulders. Sometimes there may be smaller issues containing the same amount of weight and desire the same amount of attention as larger issues in our lives. The way an issue could shape you and the amount of relief you assume you will gain by ridding yourself of certain issues creates an illusion. That illusion persuades us to relieve ourselves of a burden that seems so heavy. It gives us the perception that we are getting rid of a noticeable issue that has weighed us down. Not lifting and determining the weight of all of our burdens could have deceptively shaped our path. We characteristically choose the issue that places the largest amount of weight on our life decisions. Those decisions can ultimately create the illusions we have dealt with major issues. We miss the fact that the heavier issues may be the issues that appear to be the smallest and lightest. Are we seeing and weighing our life clearly? How have our perceptions on life been shaped from society? How can that perception shape other generations? How can we be SHAPED?

Sculpted

We and others (parents, relatives, friends, media, etc.) carve out figures and dimensions (lifestyles, role models) in hopes of one day becoming a work of art. The images and illusions we create, molds our perceptions of what we should be molded into. If we are unique in our own way, why do we continue to conform to the prepackaged perceptions of mankind? No altered image in a magazine or on the internet should be the model for what we aspire to look like. The true sculptor is God.

Yet you, Lord, are our Father. We are the clay, you are the potter; we are all the work of your hand.

Isaiah 64:8, NIV

Hewed

To be hewed is to be shaped with forcible cutting blows, or to be chopped or hacked into a shape. We experience this shaping through the struggles we face in life. Decisions and circumstances can allow mental and physical blows to reshape the mold you were created to be. Traumatic experiences, mental or physical abuse from others, and social dysfunction can create blemishes that will never be repaired or reformed.

They discipline us for a little while as they thought best; but God disciplines us for our good, that we may share in his holiness. No discipline seems pleasant at the time, but painful. Later on however, it produces a harvest of righteousness and peace for those who have been trained by it.

Hebrews 12:10-11, NIV

Adapted

With all the pressures of what is deemed acceptable to others, we conform to fit the image others place on us to become suitable to our social economical requirements or conditions. Decisions to adjust our desires positions us to become comfortable in being a part of purposes connected to the general human consensus, possibly relinquishing our directional purpose. We would rather be adaptable to what is acceptable by many, than live true to what brings us purposeful integrity.

> *See to it that no one takes you captive by philosophy and empty deceit according to human tradition and the basic principles of this world rather than on Christ.*
>
> Colossians 2:8, NIV

Produced

Creation's desire is to reproduce. Production of goods, resources, and values establish longevity for a perspective society viewed more influential or a necessity to continue the status quo. This mindset encourages certain groups to predetermine what will be created to shape individual perspectives on purpose and persuades conforming.

Humanity is being manufactured to reproduce our embedded conformed perceptions within the next generations. We are manufacturing generations, our children, that only reproduce with an assembly line mentality; accepting the thoughts, feelings, lifestyles, and beliefs as truth. Choosing to accept the views that the unknown majority (profiting corporations, money driven individuals, government entities,...) decides is beneficial to all, manipulating us to lose the nature to produce creatively as individuals.

Am I now trying to win the approval of men, or of God? Or am I trying to please men? If I were still trying to please men, I would not be a servant of Christ.

Galatians 1:10, NIV

Embodied

Throughout life we are bombarded with the question of representation. Who are you for? Who are you against? Which team do you like? Are you democrat or republican? Ultimately, we have been convinced that we have to identify one another through what our representations stand for, demonstrate, or exemplify. Our characterization of each other, shapes not only our views of who is being characterized, but our views of ourselves. We are persuaded to embody what is popular until it is no longer trending. You cannot STAND, if you have no STANDard.

The eye is the lamp of the body. If your eyes are good, your whole body will be full of light. But if your eyes are bad, your whole body will be full of darkness. If then the light within you is darkness, how great is that darkness!

Matthew 6:22-23, NIV

Defined

How often do we journey through life feeling everything we do or say is defined by forces unfamiliar with us? The idea of putting us in a box places restraints on nature striving to break free. Defining can either encourage discovered purpose or make search for existence confusing. Living with the predetermined notion that an individual is or will become something they have not been provided the opportunity to choose, can neutralize the passion waiting to be birthed within an individual. We do not determine each other's height, weight, or image. So, trying to define each other or be defined through the eyes of ignorance is premature.

Do not judge, or you too will be judged. For in the same way you judge others, you will be judged, and with the measure you use, it will be measured to you. "Why do you look at the speck of sawdust in your brother's eye and pay no attention to the plank in your own eye? How can you say to your brother, 'Let me take the speck out of your eye,' when all the time there is a plank in your own eye? You hypocrite, first take the plank out of your own eye, and then you will see clearly to remove the speck from your brother's eye.

Matthew 7:1-5, NIV

There are numerous ways we can be shaped into what we identify as "me." Regardless of what has shaped us, we must make a conscious and thoughtful attempt to navigate our lives to what our true self is. In Mark 14, there is a story about a young man that was following Jesus at the time He was arrested, due to being betrayed by Judas.

A young man, wearing nothing but a linen garment, was following Jesus. When they seized him, he fled naked, leaving his garment behind.

Mark 14:51-52, NIV

The highlight of this scripture is, of course, the young man fled naked. What might be the significance of this unidentified young man? What message can we gather from him fleeing naked?

I would suggest that when following Jesus, we should reveal our true vulnerable self, not just to Him, but also for others to see. Now wait!

I'm not recommending getting naked in front of people. I'm recommending being open to being vulnerable. Let others get to know your testimony. Jesus knows what is under our garments. Displaying vulnerability in the midst of others, identifies we are following Him and are visibly separated from a conforming society.

Keeping our clothes on and blending in with society is why we have been shaped in a way that is unidentifiable to those seeking a relationship with God. When we expose our inner selves to the world, acknowledging we are followers of Jesus Christ, it will allow your personal relationship to develop with God. It will provide those seeking purpose to understand what benefits they will obtain by becoming a part of the body of Christ. Witnessing a physical example will encourage them to seek a personal relationship with God, unveiling the ramifications of being connected to this corrupt world, and position them to receive guidance to their created purpose.

A physical infant desires to be fed, developed, and shaped by their biological parents. That connection is exemplified by the likeness displayed by the parents and infants to the outside world.

Within our infant stage of Christianity, we must choose who we will allow to feed us, which influences our choices of who will shape and develop us. As children, numerically speaking, we lack the authority to choose, but we have no excuse as adults. Life provides the choice to cultivate a relationship with the world or cultivate a relationship with God. This choice will determine whether our path is in line with how society desires us to live, or in line with our created purpose. What must be understood is that transitioning into the next stage of Christian development cannot take place unless we disconnect from the clutches of society, acknowledge God as our provider, and plan out our lives to be an example for Christ for others.

Gadfly Moments:

• *Are you alive or just living?*

• *I know lifting all of your burdens can be heavy, but have you tried lifting up the Savior? He will lift those burdens for you.*

Infant Stage Life Application

1. Evaluate and identify who or what has been feeding your development. Determine whether you have been fed properly, allowing for progressive development or dependency.

2. Figure out what you have been fed and what type of influence that information has had on the decisions you've made. Pinpointing the healthy or unhealthy nature of that information could be instrumental in confirming or redirecting your path.

3. Decide whether you are prepared for transitioning from the infant stage to toddler stage. Determine if you have been instructed on how to feed yourself. Knowledge of the necessary tools and how to properly use those tools will be critical when developing into a toddler.

Spiritual Development: Toddler Stage

I write to you, little children, because your sins are forgiven you for His name's sake.

1 John 2:12, NIV

Some Christians grow to be little children spiritually, but stop there. They often are untruthful, envious, and cruel. If rebuked, they are resentful and often make a scene. They are tattletales and loud mouths, and like gossipers, repeating everything they hear. They give into emotional outbursts, and are easily puffed up. They love praise, will accept it from any source, and will seek only the things that appeal to "self."

Chapter 3

Do You Have the Tools?

I remember being a teenager, impatiently waiting to become an adult. One question I wondered as a young man was what it took to be an adult, especially how to be a man! The most important aspect I have learned in adulthood is being equipped with the tools you need when necessary.

With the numerous situations and circumstances we will face in life, having the right tools to deal with the twist and turns of life will assist with stabilizing us. The problem with some of us is we would rather react after situations occur rather than take actions to prepare. Preventing or reducing the effects of situations, if or when they occur, is a sign of maturity.

My family and I were on the tail end of the one year lease in an apartment. We were easing through the beginning of 2014 when, in March, I got injured at work. I suffered a hernia and needed surgery immediately. It was not easy for me to wrap my mind around having to be sedated, cut open, and stitched up, but I had no other choice. This was the first real surgery I had ever experienced. Life got serious for me! I understood it was a minor surgery, but the fear of a possible mishap made me uncomfortable.

I contemplated the possibility of something going wrong. I knew I hadn't planned enough to make sure my family was taken care of if something happened to me. Surgery was successful, but I came home in tremendous pain with restrictions and guidelines; no lifting over five pounds, pain medication, and plenty of rest. I felt useless. One weekend, I tried lifting a gallon of milk to help with putting groceries away, but I couldn't lift it off the floor. My son, 5 years old at the time, grabbed it and put it in the refrigerator with ease. Silently, I cried when I was alone. Going through the process of anxiety earlier in the year and now dealing with recovering from surgery made me feel like I couldn't catch a break.

Recovery took six weeks. During that time I focused on letting my body heal and trusting my family would take care of the things I was accustomed to being responsible for. I realized I had equipped myself to be in control, but was not equipped to relinquish it. I had planned out security measures for my family if tragedy or mishaps occurred, but I never included them in the plans. They had no clue what I had planned or how to function within what I created. I ultimately designed it for me to control. The loneliness I discussed in the previous chapter, learning patience through healing and recognizing my struggles with relinquishing control, was equipping me for life's situations. Those stages I experienced helped with gaining the tools necessary for uncontrollable situations, and prepared me to deal with an experience that would change my family's path forever.

In May of 2014, my family was finally positioned to purchase a fixer upper home. The school year was coming to a close and we were spending countless hours remodeling the fixer upper home before we moved in. My wife was extremely excited to finish the school year because we decided this would be the year she would resign from teaching. She wanted to stay home and be more focused on family and available for our kids.

A couple of weeks before school ended, my son's demeanor changed. He went from an energetic child to one who always seemed tired and sad. It was his first year of school, so we assumed he was struggling with leaving his new friends and teacher. Kindergarten woes! My wife and I researched his behavior and was somewhat convinced he was showing signs of separation anxiety. The school year ended and he continued the same behavior. He and his sister were usually laughing, playing, and arguing all day, but he wasn't in the mood to do anything but sit around and appear heartbroken. He would display moments of energy, then go back to looking tired and sad. We were clueless and discouraged.

We began monitoring every little change in his behavior and noticed he was getting up in the middle of every night to use the bathroom. We figured he was drinking too much liquid at night, so we decided on a cut-off time for liquids at night. His late night bathroom frequency increased. My wife decided it was time to schedule an appointment with his pediatrician. I had to work the day of the appointment. I remember pacing the floor all morning waiting on some news. My wife finally called and explained she was advised to take my son to the hospital emergency room. I left work in time to meet them there. We checked in and were immediately directed to a room where nurses began hooking our son up to every monitor present in the room.

Being a licensed emergency medical technician, and being familiar with the procedures that take place in a hospital room should have prepared me for what I was witnessing, but seeing my child placed on medical devices and the unknown was hard to bear. Doctors finally arrived to inform my wife and me of my son's diagnosis, Type 1 Diabetes! It hit us hard. We hugged, we kissed, and we cried as a family. I came unglued. It was a tough moment. The emotions poured out of me at that moment. The thoughts of my son not having a normal childhood engulfed my mind. We looked at one another wondering if this was real. We had a rough night at the hospital, but were grateful we had friends and family willing to be available and helpful in our time of struggle.

There was a private moment I shared with my son while he was lying on the hospital bed. It was a moment that helped me see the changes God had orchestrated in my existence. I leaned over and whispered, "From this day forward we are going to tackle this together. I will be with you every step of the way. What you eat, I eat. What you have to do, I will do with you. I got you son."

There was a calming that came over me before I whispered it, and a confidence that came over him once he heard it. I believe this was the same dialogue God communicated to me within my stages of struggle; communication that prepared me for that moment. I also believe this is the dialogue God has with each of us, if we are listening. I came away from the moment understanding I was giving control of this change in our lives over to God, and only He would be able to give us the strength to endure it.

We left the hospital the next morning in good spirits. It was strange, but there was an understanding. God took over, and we had shifted to another stage in our walk with Him. Preparation and patience became a valuable tool and a critical process of our daily living. It continues to be how we live our lives today. Actually researching and preparing our mind, body, and soul for life changes provides us clarity and patience within uncontrollable experiences. We study and communicate to equip ourselves with the tools we feel are necessary to face the obstacles that may come.

> *In the same way, the Spirit helps us in our weakness. We do not know what we ought to pray for, but the Spirit himself intercedes for us through wordless groans. And he who searches our hearts knows the mind of the Spirit, because the Spirit intercedes for God's people in accordance with the will of God. And we know that in all things God works for the good of those who love him, who have been called according to his purpose.*
>
> *Romans 8:26-28, NIV*

Using the Wrong Tools

A number of missteps can occur when the wrong tool is utilized. When thinking of tools, a number of things come to mind. To name a few, there are machine tools, drawing tools, and digital tools. What we do recognize is, without tools, certain tasks needing to be performed would not be attempted. In some instances we have tools, but we do not have the right ones. In a world where we are measured by the tasks we perform, it is important we have the right tools on hand to perform the tasks. A tree cannot be cut with a hammer. You cannot hammer with a saw. If we don't know what we need, what we need it for, or how to use it, we are setting ourselves up for failure and to be stagnant.

Life can be a challenge with or without obstacles. Trying to figure out how to navigate it gets confusing. There was a sermon I experienced that assisted me with understanding the concepts of life. Understanding the concepts of life requires pinpointing tool selection. Life was explained as the three "T's." Life as a *Test*, *Trust*, and *Temporary Assignment*.

Having an understanding about what your life is about will help with properly equipping yourself with the right tools for the situations you will endure. In most worldly aspects of life, it makes sense to us to spend time gathering the tools necessary to perform certain tasks. We go to school to prepare for the life of working. We go to the gym for the benefits of a healthy life. Lessons or courses are created to help people become whatever they are inspired to become in life. For some reason, we spend a small amount of time gathering tools to better equip our spirit for the journey of life. Let's look at Christianity.

The Christian walk is spent going to church study groups, church rehearsals, and church events. We will average around five hours a week being involved in these areas to help develop our understanding of Christianity. That adds up to 20 hours a month and 240 hours a year, which equals up to around 10 days a year developing a genuine, in depth, stable relationship with God.

So, 10 days out of 365 days is what is considered enough time to spend with the Creator of our purpose? I know you're thinking you're in church more than that, so let's add a couple more days to satisfy your pride. I understand we are busy with worldly living, but how can we equip ourselves with 10 days a year?

Children go to school around 180 days a calendar year, per grade level, to prepare themselves for the careers they aspire to journey into when they reach adulthood. The funny thing is, a lot of Christians act like experts when it comes to being a Christian. If you say God is in your heart, why do your facial expressions say otherwise when questioned about your Godly living? Defensiveness! Anger! Cluelessness! The question we should be asking ourselves is, *what tools do I need and how do I get them?* Paul explained it this way in the book of Galatians:

So I say, walk by the Spirit, and you will not gratify the desires of the flesh. For the flesh desires what is contrary to the Spirit, and the Spirit what is contrary to the flesh. They are in conflict with each other, so that you are not to do whatever you want. But if you are led by the Spirit, you are not under the law. The acts of the flesh are obvious: sexual immorality, impurity and debauchery; idolatry and witchcraft; hatred, discord, jealousy, fits of rage, selfish ambition, dissensions, factions and envy; drunkenness, orgies, and the like. I warn you, as I did before, that those who live like this will not inherit the kingdom of God. But the fruit of the Spirit is love, joy, peace, forbearance, kindness, goodness, faithfulness, gentleness and self-control. Against such things there is no law. Those who belong to Christ Jesus have crucified the flesh with its passions and desires. Since we live by the Spirit, let us keep in step with the Spirit. Let us not become conceited, provoking and envying each other.

Galatians 5:16-26, NIV

How can we obtain the fruits of the Spirit? Tools.

Test

The first tool is to have belief in something that structures and determines your life choices. Within the duration of life we will be tested. The basis of a test is intended to establish an understanding of what we stand for or identify with. Our performance, qualities, and integrity are placed under a microscope for us, and sometimes others to judge. In the book of Mark, Peter was tested. Jesus had been arrested and Peter followed behind as Jesus was being delivered to the high priest.

Prior to this occurring, Jesus and Peter had a discussion about what was predicted to come. Jesus explained He would be leaving the disciples, putting them in a position to choose their allegiance. Jesus told Peter that once they come for Him, they would also come for those who were always seen standing with Him. Peter stated to Jesus he would stand and identify with Him no matter what was to come. Jesus said to Peter directly, "You will deny me." When the moment of identification arrived, Peter did not pass the test.

While Peter was below in the courtyard, one of the servant girls of the high priest came by. When she saw Peter warming himself, she looked closely at him. "You also were with that Nazarene, Jesus," she said. But he denied it. "I don't know or understand what you're talking about," he said, and went out into the entryway. When the servant girl saw him there, she said again to those standing around, "This fellow is one of them." Again he denied it. After a little while, those standing near said to Peter, "Surely you are one of them, for you are a Galilean." He began to call down curses, and he swore to them, "I don't know this man you're talking about." Immediately the rooster crowed the second time. Then Peter remembered the word Jesus had spoken to him: "Before the rooster crows twice you will disown me three times." And he broke down and wept.

Mark 14:66-72, NIV

When we go through tests in life, whether it's how we act in public, how we raise our children, or how we treat others assumed better or lesser than us, measurements are being taken to see how much we have or have not matured. Are you the type that flunks out not trying because you'd rather be involved with what others think? Are you the type that does just enough to get by so you can look socially normal to some, and spiritually led by others? Are you the type that wants to know your full purpose and live to your fullest created purpose despite your social approval rate? The question of how your tests are measured depends on who you desire to determine the measurements.

Trust

The next tool involves functioning with trust and being trustworthy. We have heard the familiar saying, "Trust is earned," but do we actually live our lives with that understanding? For trust to be earned, there is a process of proving integrity through the testing of our character. Referring back to the story of Peter disowning Jesus highlights the extent we sometimes go through that proves we can't be trusted. When faced with being identified with things, or someone outside of the social norm, we separate ourselves from what we know or identify as our belief. Peter was not only disowning Jesus, he was disowning the trust he confessed to having in Jesus. Meditate on Proverbs:

> *Trust in the Lord with all your heart and lean not on your own understanding; in all your ways submit to him, and he will make your paths straight.*
>
> *Proverbs 3:5-6, NIV*

Trusting in someone and someone having trust in you provides evidence of how much work each individual has performed to earn that established trust. People trust you to be who you openly portray yourself to be. Trust is a tool used to determine how much you truly care for the life you reflect and the individuals you are a reflection on.

Do you trust in the Word and what He said regarding taking care of you?

Temporary Assignment

The final tool involves focusing on others. When the idea of life is being suggested as a temporary assignment, most of us envision how we live before death, but I would like to suggest viewing it from an additional angle. For something to be temporary, it suggests it will last for a limited period of time. For something to be an assignment, there would have to be work or tasks assigned to someone as a job or a course of study. Therefore, to have a temporary assignment would involve us having a limited time to complete an assigned task.

Think about the limited time sometimes provided to affect those around you during your daily living. There is limited time for you to give substantive guidance to your children before they become adults and are in charge of their own choices. There may be limited time for you to assist a friend in mapping out their course in life. Do you allow that opportunity to slip away and assume there will be another time for it, or do you take on the task? How many assigned decisions will you disregard before you realize they are temporary? Those situations may be critical to producing substantive information that will structure your life decisions.

In a large house there are articles not only of gold and silver, but also of wood and clay; some are for special purposes and some for common use. Those who cleanse themselves from the latter will be instruments for special purposes, made holy, useful to the Master and prepared to do any good work. Flee the evil desires of youth and pursue righteousness, faith, love and peace, along with those who call on the Lord out of a pure heart.

2 Timothy 2:20-22, NIV

At some point, we must make a decision on whether we desire to navigate through our unique lives with tools collected based on assumptions, or the tools specified for us provided by God. Continuing to live our life using the tools the world recommends is choosing to fit in with the majority, unfamiliar with our specific designed path. The flesh will always desire the tools that are utilized to function within the world. We cannot operate in the spirit with the tools of the flesh. If we elect to seek the tools provided by God, we will also be utilized as a tool for others to find their path to God and to their purpose. Our eyes must be opened to the understanding that for life to be what is hoped for, we must step into the light and out of the darkness of sin.

Gadfly Moment:

- *Would you rather be a blessed mess or an unblessed mess?*

Chapter 4

Measure Twice, Cut Once

Renovation Realities! This was the name of a popular home remodeling show on a do-it-yourself network my wife and I enjoyed watching during our time living in the apartment. The show was about couples or friends taking on the tasks of renovating a particular room in their home. Each episode began with a small introduction of the individuals renovating, a quick detailed description of the project, and their projected budget. The hour long shows were encouraging, comedic, and displayed numerous teachable moments. Renovators had plans. But once walls were opened up, items were broken, or plans didn't work out, they were forced to make choices to enable their projects to be completed.

What stood out was the renovators' gradual understanding of how difficult the projects actually were, and how unprepared they were for it. There was often a need for an expert to assist. The realization that there was not enough time to complete the projects as planned, due to the unknown circumstances that transpired, provided a stress filled reality check.

The unpredictable amount of mistakes made, and tension created between individuals expressing favorable relationships throughout the episodes, created a desire to watch other episodes. There were measurements made too long or too short. Measurements were made without measurement tools. The wrong tools were used quite often. But as each project progressed, the renovators eventually learned from their mistakes, obtained the right tools, and finished the projects.

"Renovation Realities" became an example for my family's life. We were balancing our son's Type 1 Diabetes diagnosis and remodeling our recently purchased home. Yes, we were remodeling, but within that journey, I realized we were renovating the realities of our lives. It was called our "new normal." Two months was the deadline we set for us to renovate our home before moving in. Changes were needed in every room of the home, so we ripped out carpet, cabinetry, and lighting. Nothing was left, except for the acceptable exterior and interior walls that needed painting. A complete overhaul was done. Not knowing how to remodel a home, opened us up to making a number of mistakes and waste a lot of material, but the learning experience allowed us to grow in our understanding of how to properly transform our home and transform our lives, using the proper tools. Over time, we learned that making the necessary measurements prior to altering the state of the product utilized, saved us time, products, and beneficial results.

Sometimes, life is in need of a complete overhaul. Life may be acceptable, but still is in need of updates to fit where you are at specific stages in your life. Transforming your life opens us up to make mistakes, but the understanding you will gain about your life will help you grow into what was always perceived possible. You must make sure your spiritual house, YOU, serves its purpose.

Therefore, if anyone is in Christ, the new creation has come. The old has gone, the new is here!

2 Corinthians 5:17, NIV

Time for a Remodel?

Dating back to early cultures, a house was designed with various types of rooms and each room was configured to serve a purpose. Looking at the houses built today, we have become accustomed to not consider what purpose rooms serve for us and our families. Half of the rooms in homes are not used for the purpose they are intended. We have kitchens we don't cook in, dining rooms we don't eat in, and bedrooms we sometimes do not sleep in. Our house, earthly body, was created to experience different stages, evolving our purpose through our understanding of personal self and our relationship with others.

In 1 Corinthians 12:12-21 (NLV), the human body is explained in this way:

> *The human body has many parts, but the many parts make up one whole body. So it is with the body of Christ. Some of us are Jews, some are Gentiles, some are slaves, and some are free. But we have all been baptized into one body by one Spirit, and we all share the same Spirit. But our bodies have many parts, and God has put each part just where he wants it. How strange a body would be if it had only one part! Yes, there are many parts, but only one body. The eye can never say to the hand, "I don't need you." The head can't say to the feet, "I don't need you."*

This explanation provides us understanding of how vital each part of our life impacts the direction of our life and others. For us to function properly, each part must have a purpose and know how that purpose works with the other parts of the body. The way we live out our lives should mimic this concept.

Our spiritual body and physical body should function in parts for the fulfillment of one body. If certain parts of our lives do not match up with the direction or purpose of the body, it can create imbalance and confusion. Think about the rooms of a house. If there were rooms constructed with no design for purpose, would we know how to use the rooms or whether those rooms were serving their parts towards the reason the house was built? How do the rooms in a house relate to our spiritual house? Can the types of rooms in a house be viewed metaphorically to help us better understand how parts of our lives function within our purpose?

Do you not know that your bodies are temples of the Holy Spirit, who is in you, whom you have received from God? You are not your own; you were bought at a price. Therefore honor God with your bodies.
1 Corinthians 6:19-20, NIV

Bedrooms (A Personal Testimony)

Bedrooms are intended for rest, but also used for privacy. It's a place where we can hide our true image and rejuvenate our body after the personal struggles of a laboring day. The bedroom provides us a safe haven to strip off what we have covered up from others, but allows us to regain our strength to journey into an unforgiving world to exemplify an identity of our choosing. It is where we are most vulnerable and able to put our egos to bed. We are able to evaluate our in-depth relationship with God, one on one. The rejuvenation of our mind and spirit is strengthened, allowing us to expose our vulnerabilities to those individuals God positions in our lives to be examples for.

Bathrooms (Rebirth/Transformation)

These rooms contain the appliances and accessories for cleansing of the flesh and for forming the image we want others to see. This is where we can put our face on! The cleansing and transformation process consistently happens within this room, providing us a fresh outlook on life. From rinsing off the dirt that has been collected, to wiping tears we have shed, we leave this room imagining a cleaner slate. You are provided the opportunity to renew your mind and body, so others see what God sees. Bathing symbolizes the death and rebirth of the spirit.

Kitchen (Faith)

This room is structured for the creation of meals to nourish the body. It also stores the substances, tools, and food needed for taking something from an inedible state to a satiable state. The substances present within a kitchen are invisible alone, but once they are combined together, it results in a satisfying mixture. You can't see a cake in its completed state when you're gathering all the ingredients, but you know the end result will be a cake. You may not be able to see the things you go through as being worth the struggle or time, but when you mix those experiences together, you will find God's merciful hand all over it.

Dining Room (Fellowship)

Time to eat? Dining rooms are separate spaces designed for individuals, families, or familiar groups to gather and consume meals. Time can sometimes be spent sharing reflections of daily activities and promoting social communication between biological and desirable close relationships. The atmosphere is open for perceptions and views to be discussed, allowing each person present to gain personal perspective and guidance on life. You are able to share the love and guidance God has provided you, with those you love and care for. We must fellowship with God and others to gain wisdom and perspective.

Living Room (Witnessing)

The living room is intended for planned social activities. It is the primary area where guests are welcomed and conversations take place with the focus of determining whether similar viewpoints about life exist. It is a comfortable and relaxing domain that provides persons the opportunity to discuss perspectives and beliefs about life with an objective and persuasive purpose. Sharing with guests allows you to share your ideas about life and express an understanding of a relationship with God, which allows them to identify what living as a child of God is like. We must be a witness by the way we live and by telling others that we witness a change in ourselves.

Closets (Prayer/Repentance)

A closet is one of the smallest rooms, but recognized as the most important. Closets are used for hanging and storing personal products. All of our clothing and personal necessities are stored for us to use and reuse. Who we choose to portray on the exterior is stored in this room. In this room, you are able to hang up burdens and store the influential steps you take each day. From the clothing you wear, the shoes you put on your feet, to the sheets you use to cover your bed with, closets hold items that remind you of your accomplishments and mistakes. The wear and tear of your life sits in closets waiting to be used, thrown away, or donated. This is the place where you can take those burdens off the hangers and shelves, and pray to a loving Almighty God.

Breaking down the possible role each room serves within a house can provide a template for how each aspect of our lives should be working together to function harmoniously for one body. If someone visits your home, what would they think of you? Does your home tell the proper story about who you are or who you are striving to become? Do the images on your walls or the clothing within the closet reflect purpose, or do they reveal a desire to blend in with social perceptions?

Here are some steps for analysis:

1. Personally identify parts of your life by digging into the depths of what may have been made private, allowing you to discover circumstances that may have shaped you.

2. Decisions must be made to establish a path of character and integrity. Do you change how you live to fit who you want to be, change who you are to fit how you want to live, or stay the same?

3. Figure out your belief system so your actions will line up with your choices.

4. Reevaluate the presence of the influencers in your life and whom should be trusted with being a part of or informed with your life experiences.

5. Be in constant prayer, seeking forgiveness for the decisions you will make as you navigate through life.

Minimalism has become a trend for individuals in the 21st century. The technique of minimalism involves the focus of living a simplistic life by making sure everything you have has purpose for being in your life. Your life as a Christian should display that same focus. Every aspect of life should be set up as an example of the life we are pursuing - the way we live, the places we go, the way we interact with others. There should be a portrayal or developing of the truth we believe in.

I took a class in college called "Creative Discovery." We drew pictures, colored, and made crafts. The class put an imprint on my life. The instructor encouraged us to get back to the basics of learning and pushed us to examine the rationality behind our creativity. She explained how as children we are taught to restrict our creativity to the confines of the structured, accepted adult familiarities. We are molded to color inside the lines, but our nature is to be free to express our inner creativity. There is a time to stay within the lines and a time to let go and explore outside the boundaries.

With passion, she expressed how we would find ourselves within our "niche." Finding our "niche" involved us tapping into our innermost being of creativity, almost childlike basics, and lumping that with what your life seems to always migrate to. If you seem to always take the form of a teacher in most environments, teaching is your niche. If serving is what you are drawn to, serving is your niche. It's that thing you love to do that permeates into every part of your life.

If we desire to build our house in a way that is conducive, understanding ourselves and developing a relationship with God, we must decide whose purpose we are living for. Every part of life plays a role in providing us direction to life's worth. We cannot function with one purpose while sending mixed signals. We're either seeking our direction or piggybacking off the directions of others. Our spiritual house should be designed for the spirit of God to reside within it.

"Now fear the Lord and serve him with all faithfulness. Throw away the gods your ancestors worshiped beyond the Euphrates River and in Egypt, and serve the Lord. But if serving the Lord seems undesirable to you, then choose for yourselves this day whom you will serve, whether the gods your ancestors served beyond the Euphrates, or the gods of the

Amorites, in whose land you are living. But as for me and my household, we will serve the Lord." Then the people answered, "Far be it from us to forsake the Lord to serve other gods!"

Joshua 24:14-16, NIV

Direction in life will be confusing unless a line is drawn.

Draw a Line

In the previous chapter, I referenced life being about the three T's. There is a fourth "T" that I believe is associated with those areas, and can be viewed as more critical. Life is "Temptation." To prevent temptation from redirecting the life that was designed for you, a choice has to be made. Let's do some spiritual math. If a negative (worldly) and a negative (self) is added together, you still get a negative (flesh). But, if a positive (Spirit) and a negative (you) are added together, you get a positive (Spirit). But, there can be a kink in this math. If the negatives (self and worldly) are more concentrated than the positive (Spirit), the added together outcome is negative (flesh).

Those who live according to the flesh have their minds set on what the flesh desires; but those who live in accordance with the Spirit have their minds set on what the Spirit desires. The mind governed by the flesh is death, but the mind governed by the Spirit is life and peace. The mind governed by the flesh is hostile to God; it does not submit to God's law, nor can it do so. Those who are in the realm of the flesh cannot please God.

Romans 8:5-8, NIV

My grandfather explained making choices on a napkin when he was providing my wife and I marriage counseling. The process explained can be difficult if you are still in the mindset of living your life for self-preservation. I was not ready at the time, but finally made my choice, so I could begin to live purposefully.

Let's do the exercise right now. Grab a sheet of paper.

1. Draw a line down the center of your paper.

2. On one side of the paper, draw two large circles. (Big enough to write your thoughts in.)

3. Using one or two words, write in one circle the struggles you have dealt with in your life.

4. In the other circle, write the people of influence (good or bad) in your life.

5. Once you have completed the circles, draw one big circle on the other side of the line. Write God and your name in that circle.

6. This is where you have to make a decision. Evaluate what was written in the two other circles, and decide which persons and struggles should be transferred in the circle with you and God.

What this process does is provides a visual of how you could have gotten off track, who has been influencing your journey, and a possible reason why God has not been able to keep your intentions in line with your purpose. There is a truth about the temptations you face in life. Temptations are not there by accident. I understand we have a sense that God is constantly testing us and involved in these struggles somehow, but I would ask you to consider this.

When tempted, no one should say, "God is tempting me." For God cannot be tempted by evil, nor does he tempt anyone; but each person is tempted when they are dragged away by their own evil desire and enticed. Then, after desire has conceived, it gives birth to sin; and sin, when it is full-grown, gives birth to death. Don't be deceived, my dear brothers and sisters. Every good and perfect gift is from above, coming down from the Father of the heavenly lights, who does not change like shifting shadows. He chose to give us birth through the word of truth, that we might be a kind of firstfruits of all he created.

James 1:13-18, NIV

The temptations we experience are orchestrated by our willingness to keep living a life comfortable with struggling to find truth through our own lens. *Can you change your life for the better by following the same routine?* Temptations will not decrease unless the decision is made to diminish and nullify the decisions that have kept those temptations relevant in your life.

We must outsmart ourselves and make changes to steer clear of bad choices. We desire to measure ourselves with each other, which creates a measuring of ignorance. That mindset involves functioning and making decisions as though 24/7 monitoring of others' lives is attainable. The attachments some of us have to social networks has cultivated a nature to keep track of the lives of others while neglecting our own life. We must focus on choosing the path and methods that fit our life. You cannot create the best days of your life by following methods that have resulted in the worst days of your life. Understanding your development spiritually will provide clarity for readiness to move to the next stage. Identifying your struggles and temptations, shifts your mindset from masking your faults to becoming a testimony for others to witness. No longer will your focus be about boasting to the world so you can be recognized. Life will transform into a quest to find out who God is, how God can assist you with figuring out who you are to become, and then witness to others who God is and who He can be for them. We can continue to disclose information directed towards the uplifting of our ego and overshadow personal shortcomings, or utilize information gathered for beneficial character and relationship development. I will end with a quote from my grandmother, "There is no right way to be wrong!"

Gadfly Moments:

• *Are you tempted to live right or are you tempted to be tempted?*

• *Are you making choices based on your temptations or based on who you hope to become?*

• *Are your temptations delaying your journey?*

Toddler Stage Life Application

1. Determine whether you want your level of knowledge and Christianity to grow or stay put.

2. Decide if you care more about the image you have established with those around you and social influences, or would you rather your image be structured and in-line with a belief system deemed purposeful.

3. Evaluate your personal agendas when determining how to utilize the information disclosed to you by trusting individuals.

Spiritual Development: Young Adult Stage

"I am writing to you, fathers, because you know him who is from the beginning. I am writing to you, young men, because you have overcome the evil one."

1 John 2:13, NIV

Spiritual growth of a young adult is not reached without focus. They are strong, virile, and have a focus to overcome their strongholds. They have a vision for the future, faith, and courage to tackle it. They make preparation for productive years. You, too, can become a young adult spiritually by "doing away with childish things."

"When I was a child, I talked like a child, I thought like a child, I reasoned like a child. When I became a man, I put the ways of childhood behind me."

1 Corinthians 13:11, NIV

Chapter 5

Guess Work

During my childhood, I spent a lot of summers in Georgia with my grandfather. My grandfather, being a pastor and missionary, created an environment for numerous conversations about life and Christianity. Fortunately, there were discussions of how life and Christianity could be synonymous when prioritized.

My grandparents had a screened in back deck that I enjoyed relaxing on, but dreaded the discussions I would endure. There were discussions that rendered me speechless and quite confused. Within those discussions on the deck, my grandfather had an unconventional way of knowing what was going on in my life and where my life was headed, based on the directions I expressed. The confusing part was him knowing me without me telling him the truth. I assumed there was some communication with my mother, but most of the information was personal secrets. I would wonder how he knew so much about my life, but was intimidated to ask.

As I grew older, I began to piece together how he was able to picture the life of others. At a young age, my grandfather was teaching me the fundamentals of the Christian journey, but I had to be at the right stage in life to fully utilize that information to unveil purposeful steps. The relationship between my grandfather and I was challenging because of our different views on life, but even more challenging as I journeyed deeper into adulthood. I gained my own experiences and that structured my perspectives and my approaches to those perspectives. Living based on the stages of mankind are different from the developmental stages of a Christian. Mankind's view of adulthood involves age, while Christianity's view of adulthood involves the level of relationship with God.

One interaction fractured our relationship. He was visiting Nashville and requested my brother and me to help him empty out some ministry materials he had stored in a storage unit while he was on a mission trip in Africa. He knew that I had a Suburban, so the plan was to load this material in my vehicle. There were some large file cabinets he wanted to take with him, but I felt the cabinets were too large to fit in the

Suburban. I explained to him that they were too long and would not fit, but he was adamant that those cabinets be taken.

The exchange can be summarized this way. *"They won't fit."* He responded with, *"How do you know?"* I explained, with my "treat-me-as-an-adult" ego, that it was my vehicle and I knew what would or would not fit. His response was, *"Did you measure it?"* I decided to prove how much I knew and measured them. They did fit! My ego took a huge hit and put a strain on our relationship that lasted for years. My ego got in the way. Making decisions by guessing proved my knowledge.

During the time my family was going through changes, my grandfather was wrapping up his mission work in Africa. Communication began to slowly increase, and our once fractured relationship was on a road to recovery. I recall contacting my grandfather about my son's Type 1 Diabetes diagnosis and discussing the struggles to come. He stated to me with resolve, "Your son has you." I was reminded of what I was taught on that screened deck and it began to make more sense.

One of my purposes was to guide my children by providing them the fundamentals of a Christian life, and also to assist them in understanding that their purpose in life will be obtained if they decide to dig deeper, not guess, for knowledge and understanding of God. That understanding is how my grandfather knew my living footprints. He was teaching me the similarities mankind has in one another, and the lives we are all choosing to live. I was taught to measure my life by the requirements of my Heavenly Father, so I could make a decision between life in the Spirit or death through the flesh. That could only be reached by constantly reading, studying, researching, praying, and meditating on what I choose to be the ruler of my life. No guessing!

Hypothesis

A hypothesis is defined as an assumption or concession made for the sake of an argument. An educated guess! It is viewed as a tentative assumption made in order to draw out and test its logical or experiential consequences. A subconscious internal standard must be established, so guessing will not be used just to avoid being questioned. The key word, when defined, and primary principle in a hypothesis is that the assumptions or concessions are "tested." We must go through a process of testing our guesses. Testing your guesses builds knowledge within the areas questioned. Questioning yourself provides confidence in expressing truths within areas that are consistent or similar to the areas you have already gained factual understanding in. Not defining your truth within the context of misinformation can be detrimental to what you perceive to be foundational truths to live by.

How should we gain a better understanding of the things we are unfamiliar with and live our lives questioning? First, you must determine what is preventing you from discontinuing the mindset of guarding yourself from the feeling of ignorance and be open to acknowledging what you do not understand. Second, you must decide whether you would like to be enlightened or continue a self-imposed path of being unquestioned. Finally, a decision has to be made of whether what is being questioned will affect the direction of the generation that is influenced by you. Each questionable truth should be taken through a process of experimentation. That process in science is called the scientific method. The scientific method is a process for experimentation that is used to explore observations and answer questions. I implore you to practice this method to reinvent your perception. The process involves systematic observation, measurement, and experimentation, and the formulation, testing, and modification of the hypotheses.

I know you are wondering how science can be utilized to assist you with your understanding of your purpose. What you must be is intentional when utilizing this method and you will ultimately identify how perceptive guessing has hindered your productive growth into your purpose. Let's look at the steps and how these steps can be applied.

Identify the Question

The method begins with questioning. In a purposeful sense, it begins with questioning oneself. We must constantly ask ourselves what we believe, why do we believe it, how has that belief affected our decision making, and what circumstances may be preventing us from beneficial change. We must not be stubborn to our beliefs. Questioning our stances of existence allows proper maturing of mind, body, and soul.

Gather Information

This step involves diligent and in-depth research. Locating factual information to either confirm or reconstruct your understanding of critical elements of life is instrumental to making choices. Navigating through life based on the uninformed premature choices of others can lead you into a path of delusion.

Hypothesis

The educated guess is examined. What was once a foundational belief or understanding has to be proven. Our choices have to be placed under a microscope and analyzed as to how we came upon our decision. Our prediction has to be measured for overall success. Can you make a valid argument to stand on the choices you make?

Experiment

This step invites you to test, evaluate, reexamine, and determine whether your choices provide positive results or conditions need to be modified. This is the area where you have the opportunity to eliminate some factors that have been identified as altering preconceived results. Choices have to be questioned and researched for us to evaluate whether our choices are working. Looking over the choices we've made with the intention to improve on the missteps of our infancy allows us to mature graciously and gracefully.

Draw a Conclusion

The final step to this process is determining results and communicating those results to others. What was once a guess without validity, becomes a knowledgeable choice for your path and for others to utilize for their journey. The conclusion is not finite, but purposeful within each stage of development. The totality of the conclusion can and will not be met until we are mature enough to handle the unadulterated truth. Each evaluated choice discloses understanding conducive to the stage of life prepared for.

> *Do not quench the Spirit. Do not despise prophecies, but test everything; hold fast what is good.*
>
> *1 Thessalonians 5:19-21, ESV*

But let him ask in faith, with no doubting, for the one who doubts is like a wave of the sea that is driven and tossed by the wind.

James 1:6, ESV

Utilizing steps, such as the scientific method, can assist you with better determining why your truth is your truth and whether your truth is actually truth. Desiring to live with purpose requires each of us to pursue deeper uncomfortable meanings of life and not settle for the sugar coated perceptions we've grown accustomed to measuring purpose by.

Gadfly Moments:

• *Are you guessing through life or are you confident in the decision you are making for yourself?*

• *Is guessing your way protecting your ignorance or is it your way of avoiding change?*

• *Do you question others, but do not see yourself as needing to be questioned?*

Chapter 6

No Quick Fixes

If I were to ask you what most people desire when they are faced with a problem, what would be the dominant answer? A quick fix! We are living in a time where we want things done quickly, or it is viewed as a disappointment. No longer is it favorable to display patience in a society that promotes instant gratification. Food now! Illnesses healed now! Education now! Spiritual experience now! This mindset has developed a nature that does not provide us the attitude to develop physically, morally, or spiritually.

The lack of developmental patience eliminates proper understanding of how to gradually shift into the stages of life. No longer do we teach others how to patiently wait so they can handle the changes life will bring. Those with experience in the possible missteps when not being patient have also bought into the mindset of needing a quick fix. Society promotes the notion of finding ways to skip the "process." There are steps and stages we must go through. I believe there is a reason most of us do not know where we are going in life, and how to stay there once we reach our destination. We are not paying attention to the process of how gathering knowledge assists in sustaining a progressive understanding. What are we missing? In the book of Matthew, Jesus highlights the reason we continue to lack full understanding of our life.

Then Jesus went with his disciples to a place called Gethsemane, and he said to them, "Sit here while I go over there and pray." He took Peter and the two sons of Zebedee along with him, and he began to be sorrowful and troubled. Then he said to them, "My soul is overwhelmed with sorrow to the point of death. Stay here and keep watch with me." Going a little farther, he fell with his face to the ground and prayed, "My Father, if it is possible, may this cup be taken from me. Yet not as I will, but as you will." Then he returned to his disciples and found them sleeping. "Couldn't you men keep watch with me for one hour?" he asked Peter. "Watch and pray so that you will not fall into temptation. The spirit is willing, but the flesh is weak." He went away a second time and prayed, "My Father, if it is not possible for this cup to be taken away unless I drink it, may your will be done." When he came back, he again found them sleeping, because their eyes were heavy. So he left them and went away once more and prayed the third time, saying the same thing. Then he returned to the disciples and said to them, "Are you still sleeping and resting? Look, the hour has come, and the Son of Man is delivered into the hands of sinners. Rise! Let us go! Here comes my betrayer!"

Matthew 26:36-46, NIV

There are statements within these scripture verses that highlight the processes Jesus wants us to understand for proper physical, moral, and spiritual development.

Physical:

"Stay here and keep watch with me."

The time for Jesus to be arrested was coming and Jesus requested for the disciples to watch their surroundings while He wrestled with His purpose. This was a request the disciples should have been prepared for. Jesus consistently spoke of the time when He would be betrayed, and expressed to the disciples their need to decide whether they would stand with him once the prophecy occurred. The disciples' visions were being tested during this time. They were asked to stay vigilant for anyone and anything that would disrupt the process Jesus was experiencing. Jesus was visually taking them through the physical process of preparing for purpose.

The perception of life through Christ and death through sin cannot be identified unless we visually identify life experiences. It is through our eyes that we decipher right and wrong. If we do not keep a visual watch for the things that are coming or happening, we set ourselves up for missing critical situations that will assist us with making purposeful life decisions.

Moral:

"Watch and pray so that you will not fall into temptation."

Before this statement was made, Jesus returned to the disciples to find them sleeping. He asked them to keep watch, but their flesh was not willing to stay awake. Jesus went off to pray a second time, but made sure to emphasize the power of prayer while He was away. Jesus emphasized the role of prayer for the purpose of teaching them how to keep their flesh in check. He knew their flesh would struggle with staying strong, so He provided them another tool to assist with the mental struggles. The mind of the disciples was being tested and prayer was identified as a resource to combat that struggle.

We too struggle with mental battles that constantly engulf our lives from day to day. The way we view society and make decisions as to what is right and wrong, creates a tangled mess within our existence. Not properly identifying what we are seeing or not seeing can be even more debilitating. Is perception reality? The nature of temptation creates that web of entanglement. Strengthening of our existence will be absorbed through the observation of life experiences (watch), and the utilization of safeguards (prayer) designed to protect us when in need. These tools are not only used when struggles happen, but should consistently be practiced to regulate us through all life. We must have morals to live by or we will fall victim to immorality. Defending yourself with positive tools is key.

Spiritual:

Then he returned to the disciples and said to them, *"Are you still sleeping and resting?"*

Finally, Jesus left a third time to pray, only to return and find his disciples sleeping and resting. Because of their lack of attentiveness, they were not prepared for the arrival of the soldiers and betrayer, or prepared for the decisions needed to be made now that their spiritual leader had been taken away. If we were to read further, we would find that the disciples separated and scattered throughout the city, trying to grapple with the change that was predicted by Jesus. They were also struggling to retain the teaching He instilled in each of them to grasp onto.

There is a word that I feel is most evident when Jesus was speaking to His disciples prior to the betrayal. He asked if they were *still* sleeping. *Still* meaning they were sleeping most, if not the whole time they were supposed to be watching and praying. I believe He is expressing the cause for spiritual disconnection. We walk around in a constant drowsy state. Being in a constant drowsy state creates a life where we walk around with our eyes mostly closed and our consciousness separated from reality. Our impressions on life are based upon the illusions that are created, which are produced by the small amount of imagery that is present to the desires of the flesh. We must be fully awake to see all that is behind and in front of us. Our belief in assuming we can fully comprehend and operate while indulging in sleep behavior explains why we cannot obtain the understanding or knowledge required to connect with the soul God created within us. There are no quick fixes in the path of your life. If a quick fix is what you want or have tried, you will likely find out that the fix will not be sustainable. Waking up and being present is most important in the development of a substantial relationship with God. That process will prepare you to wrestle with the weakening of the flesh, strengthen your prayer life, and provide you a deeper connection with God.

Therefore do not become partners with them; for at one time you were darkness, but now you are light in the Lord. Walk as children of light (for the fruit of light is found in all that is good and right and true), and try to discern what is pleasing to the Lord. Take no part in the unfruitful works of darkness, but instead expose them. For it is shameful even to speak of the things that they do in secret. But when anything is exposed by the light, it becomes visible, for anything that becomes visible is light. Therefore it says,
"Awake, O sleeper, and arise from the dead, and Christ will shine on you." Look carefully then how you walk, not as unwise but as wise, making the best use of the time, because the days are evil. Therefore do not be foolish, but understand what the will of the Lord is."

Ephesians 5:7-17, NLT

Gadfly Moments:

• *You don't sleep much when your desires are the focus. Why do you seem so tired when God is the focus?*

• *What are you missing out on by sleeping through what is critical to your development?*

• *Are you encouraging others to sleep or to stay "awake"?*

Chapter 7

It's Not Level

Having balance in life is the goal for most of us. With work, schedules, and other interests consuming my family's time, we assumed our life was balanced out. Something common became a constant theme in our lives. We couldn't sustain that balance. Life would be good. Then, we would experience small disruptive situations, and periodically, obstacles would get really bad. The newly remodeled home was wonderful and my family was in position financially to be balanced, but the weight of the world was still on each of our shoulders, tipping the scales. If it wasn't our old nature creeping back into our relationships causing discord, it was the transition of our two children's development. How do we or should we balance all of this stuff?

I tried reducing the amount of people in my life, getting enough sleep, eating better, and other suggestions the television experts advised. I would balance out, but I could not withstand the constant ups and downs my life was going through. I began to question the theory of balance itself. Balance would make me content for periods, but there were periods where portions of life were just too heavy. Even my spiritual life was taking a beating. I would talk to others as though I was a steady example of Christianity, but my facial expressions and actions did not match up with what I was preaching.

Life always has a way of keeping you honest. Society frames life as being difficult because we don't have enough balance. We are told we struggle because there is no balance in the way we eat, sleep, communicate, work, or play. There seems to be so many suggestions on why we should work to achieve balance, but no clear understanding of a way to stay in consistent balance. I looked into what balance was really about and to find out if there were steps to balancing I was missing. My hope was to figure out how to accurately implement what I discovered into my life. With all the concepts about what balancing life should involve, I dug deep into what would keep me steady and upright. I realized the only way to truly understand it was to define it.

Balance is defined as an even distribution of weight enabling someone or something to remain upright or steady. It involves proportioning different elements into equal portions, which stabilizes a position, preventing it from falling. Defining it confirmed the message that has been delivered to us through different communication outlets. Balance should keep our lives steady and upright. If the concept is true and the methods are valid, why is it so difficult to stay balanced? What could be missing from our concept of balancing that continues to tip the scales in an unfavorable direction? What will prevent us from constantly falling and keep us steady? Should I be shooting for the distribution of weight? In the book of Job, Job explained his struggles with balance this way:

> *"If I have walked with falsehood or my foot has burned after deceit, let God weigh me in honest scales and he will know that I am blameless."*
>
> Job 31:5-6, NIV

Job struggled through many adversities in his life. He lost everything he valued, but he stayed steady in his beliefs in God. No matter the tragedies or circumstances he faced, Job never turned his back or lost faith in the Creator. Is there a concept we must pay attention to as to how Job stayed balanced? Is there an understanding within the story of Job that kept him steady through life?

Is It Straight?

I believe there is a concept present within the story of Job that is critical to staying balanced. The concept of being "level." When remodeling parts of my home, the most important tool I used was a leveler. Without that tool, the structures and projects around my home would not bear the weight or stay upright as they should. Therefore, something must first be level before anything can be balanced. How does this concept apply to our lives?

Level is understood as a line or horizontal plane respective to a given point or distance. It involves a position on a real or imaginary scale of amount, extent, quality, or quantity. How does this coincide with balance? I believe the reasoning behind not staying balanced is that we are not level. To be level is to be straight. Weight bearing is key to establishing and maintaining balance, which affects how straight something becomes. Imagine a trapeze artist. The trapeze artist is able to balance, not because of what they are doing, but because the line under them is level and straight. If the line was not level, the artist would most likely lose their balance at some point. The line will experience tension and bend when pressure is applied, but the fact that the line was leveled and straightened prior to the changes in conditions will not compromise its purpose. Along with that understanding, is realizing the line has a level path from one point to another. We must have an understanding of where we are going in life and whether the belief we are standing on is straight enough to balance our life. The problems that exist in us are; having no clue where we are going, or believing whatever new concept is trending.

Jesus replied:

> *"Every plant not planted by my heavenly Father will be uprooted, so ignore them. They are blind guides leading the blind, and if one blind person guides another, they will both fall into a ditch."*
>
> *Matthew 15:13-14, NIV*

Society's trends of instant gratification has created the nature of the unbalanced lifestyles we experience. We desire things now, and when those things are not a part of our created purpose, the scale tips to one side or the other. We are constantly teetering. We listen to the latest influential person and newest ideas, but feel it is unrealistic to consult with our Creator. Referring back to the scripture in Job, verse six states, "let God weigh me in honest scales and he will know that I am blameless." Why would he allow God to weigh him and believe he was blameless? Job was identifying the benefits of living a level life and how it was accomplished by having a relationship with God. He knew that balancing his life on the shoulders of God was keeping his scales honest and blameless. Job knew that if he stayed in line with the point God set for his life, he would not have to bear the weight that causes imbalance.

> *"Give your burdens to the LORD, and he will take care of you. He will not permit the godly to slip and fall."*
> *Psalms 55:22, NIV*

Imagine yourself on a tightrope. The main objective is to focus and walk from one side to the other. Walking on a tightrope involves you balancing on a rope or wire that is stretched between two points of emphasis. Our initial thought is that it will require a lot of work on our part to put one foot in front of the other and walk across the straight wire. The process is difficult and requires a lot of work, but we forget the tightrope is actually doing all the work to keep us level. The weight we are carrying and the points of travel exist because of the tightrope.

I would suggest that the reason we cannot stay balanced in life and lack direction is because we have no tightrope to support our weight. Recognizing it is the design of the product you are leveling is important to understanding how balancing is possible. Without allowing God to take care of your burdens and deciding to live your life for Him, you continue to live life unbalanced. God can be your tightrope.

> *"In all your ways acknowledge Him, And He will make your paths straight."*
>
> Proverbs 3:6, NIV

> *"You who are full of all deceit and fraud, you son of the devil, you enemy of all righteousness, will you not cease to make crooked the straight ways of the Lord?"*
>
> Acts 13:10, NIV

I found that balancing my life the way I chose to balance it was my way of not relinquishing the things I didn't want to give up. Really deciding to move to the next stage of my spiritual development called for me to focus on understanding my weaknesses and allowing God to care for me. He had been there all along, but to grow meant for me to submit to the path He established for me. The tightrope can bend and feel like it will give way, but the purposeful tension in the rope allows whatever is on it to stabilize. God knows that our lives will be filled with unpredictable weight, but He promises that the weight will not be more than we can balance. He can level us out as long as He is our support.

> *"So, if you think you are standing firm, be careful that you don't fall! No temptation has overtaken you except what is common to mankind. And God is faithful; he will not let you be tempted beyond what you can bear.*

But when you are tempted, he will also provide a way out so that you can endure it."

1 Corinthians 10:12-13, NIV

Gadfly Moments:

• *Are you trying to balance life to get closer to your created purpose or to make sure you can keep doing the things that keep tipping the scale?*

• *Will you ever be tired of falling, or is that a good excuse for not growing?*

Young Adult Stage Life Application

1. Determine whether you are better off guessing through life's situations or whether it's more beneficial to gain insightful knowledge about life itself.

2. Evaluate past and present quick fixes to determine if they were sustainable fixes that will not create issues down the road. Use those experiences as reference points for future decision-making. Move forward patiently, allowing an informative path to process outcomes.

3. If not balanced or balancing, create a path with the goal of balancing life's objectives and obstacles. Also, establish a line of stability to maintain that balance.

Spiritual Development: Adult Stage

"I am writing to you, fathers, because you know him who is from the beginning. I am writing to you, young men, because you have overcome the evil one."

1 John 2:13, NIV

This stage of spiritual development can be reached by all, but so few ever attain it. The spiritual adult has peace with God (Romans 5:11). Knowledge of the peace of God is understood (Philippians 4:11). They rejoice when provided knowledge of spiritual children (1 Thessalonians 2:19, 1 Timothy 1:2). They have learned contentment under all circumstances and knowledge of the only true strength (Philippians 4:11-13). There is no need for a spiritual adult to deliberate over the past, but looks to the future (Philippians 3:12-14) knowing that all things work together in life for eternal good (Romans 8:28). They enjoy abundant life now and will enjoy it in the life to come (Ephesians 2:7).

Chapter 8

Imperfect, Not Finished

It is said that perfection is in the eye of the beholder, but what does that viewpoint entail? Perfection, being dictated through the lens of humanity, is perceiving that the overall truth will not be unadulterated. There is nothing pure or nonsubjective within the minds of human beings. As adults, we learn and teach others that perfection is unattainable. What if our idea of perfection has been distorted, causing it to seem unreachable? Is the perfection we perceive based on living a faultless or flawless life accurate? Should perfection be based on living out our purpose in life by embracing our imperfections?

Some religious scholars have debated whether humanity was created perfectly based upon male and female being created in the image of God. Scripture referenced to debate perfection states,

> *Then God said, "Let us make mankind in our image, in our likeness, so that they may rule over the fish in the sea and the birds in the sky, over the livestock and all the wild animals, and over all the creatures that move along the ground." So God created mankind in his own image, in the image of God he created them; male and female he created them.*
> *Genesis 1: 26-27, NIV*

The debate revolves around whether we were created perfect and the "fall of mankind" prevents us from ever gaining perfection, or whether the notion of perfection attached to the "fall of mankind" is marked within humanity fulfilling its purpose, since God knew the fall would occur. If the fall of mankind was known by God, would He have created mankind in His image? The notion that God created us in the imagery of His perfection, knowing we were destined to be imperfect, invokes questions of what perfection may be. Let's discuss perfection from an unattainable viewpoint. When measuring our image and lives, we tend to seek the approval of others to satisfy our desires. We desire to fit in with what's considered the norm. Being unsatisfied by the answers society supplies us could be due to our nature to "project" ourselves onto others.

We perceive ourselves as sinners. The idea of "projection" is a defense mechanism that involves individuals attributing characteristics we do not like about ourselves onto others. Disapproval of ourselves makes the journey of any belief of perfection impossible. Projecting the view that perfection is only achieved by living a life free from mistakes is embedded into the minds of all mankind. Perfection is viewed unattainable from this viewpoint.

Now, let's look at perfection through the viewpoint of imperfection. What if perfection was defined as living out your purpose? What if imperfection is part of the plan? Is being imperfect perfection? When our imperfections are seen as catapulting us towards the purpose of our creation, concentration on how to properly navigate through life is developed.

Cultivating the ability to identify and correct mishaps or misdirections on our life path allows us to eliminate some errors. Eliminating errors over time diminishes the list of issues in need of repair, which casts a productive outlook on the faults that occurred, producing current situations. Being made perfect by the acknowledgement and process of working through the imperfect life we experience, alleviates the desire to only be purposeful based upon successes. So, is it perfect to be imperfect?

Our responsibility is to understand that we are being persuaded to be shaped by society, not to make decisions that will keep us on the path to purposeful living. Identifying that notion and pressing towards identifying what is best for the overall direction of our existence will keep us on track to discovering what is the key to making sure purposeful living is the end result. How can we make sure this happens? Start Over! Start over when you feel you have derailed your path to purpose. Treat each experience of enlightenment as an opportunity to allow God to tighten your tightrope, bearing the weight, which will give you the confidence to trust the direction you are pursuing.

Start Over!

I know the thought of "starting over" sounds difficult, if not impossible to do since you have gone through so much. How can I just all of a sudden change everything I do on a whim? We seem to only see changes as a possibility when we are forced by tragedy or near death experiences. The problem with that is not understanding that the decisions you may be making could be setting you up for those tragedies or near death experiences. Society convinces us we have time to mess up because products are designed to update so quickly. We also function with less stability seeing products quickly outdated, giving us the mindset we will benefit more by experiencing the next best thing.

Those illusions trick us into believing we can wait to change our life decisions. The thinking becomes, we can change when we decide to. It can happen just as fast as the products we visually see updating daily. Life doesn't work that way. We can't wait to restart, assuming it will be automatic. For some of us, it could take years to get on the track or on the path we were created for. Those gadfly moments, I have encouraged you to think about throughout this book, can assist us with restarting. Being uncomfortable is pushing us to experience new things and new directions, but forces us to seek comfort and peace in the new positions we are shifted into. Through those moments we are retooled, resourced, and enlightened to our ability to become better at being us, better at living out our purpose.

In earlier chapters, we discussed the stages of Christian development processes. It involves understanding who was feeding and shaping our early development. We identified how our early development is influenced by those we choose to model our lives after, once we mature enough to make our own decisions. Also, we analyzed how we utilize our decision making authority to establish a belief system by maintaining the imagery of our possible misdirected early development, or deciding to choose our own individual course.

Life exerts a lot of energy, whipping us into some kind of shape, but it is the understanding of adulthood that allows us to appreciate the purpose for those experiences. Adults figure out those experiences weren't meant for just them, but for those who they will influence. They discover that they play a major part of someone else's journey to becoming whole. Acknowledgement of life experiences and starting over can be a critical step to regain focus. There is more at stake when identifying the individuals that are affected by your direction.

Accepting an unguided journey might work for you when acting as though your decisions do not affect others, but eventually those ill effects on others will become noticeable. Allow the relationship you have or continue to build with God to assist you with making decisions that will benefit your walk for the rest of your life. His love for you and the ones you care for will be unconditional and never shift when trends fade. His goal is for you to be the best you, because you are His child and that benefits the Kingdom.

> *"As the Father has loved me, so have I loved you. Now remain in my love. If you keep my commands, you will remain in my love, just as I have kept my Father's commands and remain in his love. I have told you*

this so that my joy may be in you and that your joy may be complete. My command is this: Love each other as I have loved you. Greater love has no one than this: to lay down one's life for one's friends. You are my friends if you do what I command. I no longer call you servants, because a servant does not know his master's business. Instead, I have called you friends, for everything that I learned from my Father I have made known to you. You did not choose me, but I chose you and appointed you so that you might go and bear fruit—fruit that will last—and so that whatever you ask in my name the Father will give you. This is my command: Love each other."

John 15:9-17, NIV

Gadfly Moments:

• *Do you care if you are perfect or even close to perfection? Which perfection do you seek - the world's view, peoples' view, your view, or God's view?*

• *Are you trying to be perfect because perfection is your goal, belief, or purpose?*

• *Are your imperfections imperfect enough to allow a perfect God to work on you?*

Adult Stage Life Application

1. Start over daily until your decisions conform to purpose-driven beliefs identified.

2. Take an account of the effects you have on the path of others, and position yourself to operate consistently in that part.

3. Duplicate your change or adaptation by sharing your knowledge to others, allowing them to reap the benefits of your life experiences.

Final Thoughts:

- If after reading this you feel your life is in order, I pray that your life continues to be a blessing to you and others.

- If you read this book and it has affected you in a way that you feel you are in need to recommit yourself to Christ, let us pray this prayer together:

"Heavenly Father, I recommit my life to you today, and ask that you guide my steps from this day forth. I acknowledge to you that I have sinned, but I plan this day to follow your ways, knowing that you are the Way and the Life that will unveil to me my purpose in life. This I pray, In Jesus' name. AMEN!"

- If you have not committed your life to Christ, I would like to offer this opportunity to you at this time. Please read through "A Plan of Salvation" on the following pages.

Thank you for allowing me to share my life experiences, and my belief in Christ with you!

PLAN OF SALVATION

Plan: A method or way of doing something.

Salvation: Deliverance from sin and the penalty of sin.

Step 1:

Believe - to trust, to have faith in and to have total confidence in someone or something

What you must believe in order to be saved:

1. Believe there is only one true God. *(Genesis 1:1)*
2. Believe that Jesus Christ is the Son of God. *(Luke 1:35)*
3. Believe in the miraculous birth of Jesus. *(Luke 1:26-38, Luke 2:11)*
4. Believe that Jesus Christ died on the cross for the sins of all who would have faith in Him. *(Luke 23:44-46)*
5. Believe in the burial of Jesus Christ. *(Luke 23:50-56)*
6. Believe in the resurrection of Jesus Christ.

(Luke 24:1-8, Matthew 28:5-7, Mark 16:9-14, John 20:15-20)

Step 2:

Repent - a change of mind about your life and the sinful ways you are living. It is a turning to God by faith in Jesus Christ for the rest of your life.

• We must turn our back on Satan and the way he is using sin, and not rebel against God.
• We must become tired of our old life of sin, the shame and disgrace it has brought upon us.
• We must desire a new life in Jesus Christ who loves you so much.
(Luke 13:3-5, Acts 2:38, 1 John 1:9)

God is waiting on you to turn to Him!

Step 3:

Conversion - an act of God that takes place when God changes you from one condition to another.

God made us for His glory, and when we repent, He will change us from sinner to saint (Christian) to be used by Him. Always remember, God created us and He loves us, but He will not change us against our will.

Step 4:

Baptism - a ceremony commanded by Jesus, by which Christians make public confession that they have repented of their sins and have commit- ted, in faith, to Jesus as their Savior and Lord.

Spiritual baptism is an act of God rendered by the Holy Spirit. When you accept Jesus Christ as personal Savior, The Holy Spirit comes into your life immediately. Water baptism is a symbol to you and the entire world of the change that has taken place in your life spiritually. It is a spiritual act that says, *"I have made Jesus my choice, I have accepted Him as my personal Lord and Savior, and from this day forward I will live for him. I belong to Jesus!" (Luke 2:41, John 1:32-34)*

It is Decision Time!

If you have made a decision to give your life to Jesus Christ, now is the time. Do not delay. Please understand, it does not matter how long you have been a member of any church or if you were baptized with water. Water cannot wash your sins away. Only the blood of Jesus Christ, the crucified Lamb of God, can wash away sins. You must be born again!

Will you turn yourself in today? Tomorrow is not promised to you!

If you are ready to be saved, pray this prayer:

Heavenly Father, I am a sinner. I want to be saved, and I want to be forgiven for my sins. I believe Jesus died on the cross for my sins. I believe in Jesus' birth, death, and resurrection. Father, I am asking Jesus to come into my heart and save me. I thank you for accepting me into your eternal family. In the name of Jesus I pray. Amen.

Salvation, Then What?

We must be spiritually developed in order to fulfill God's plan and purpose for our life. It is wonderful to be saved, but growth normally follows birth. Find a local church group or local fellowship, and continue to grow in relationship with God through His Word.

Notes: